Contents

Aa	2
Bb	3
Cc	5
Dd	7
Ee	8
Ff	9
Gg	10
Hh	11
Ii	12
Jj	13
Kk	14
Ll	15
Mm	16
Nn	18
Oo	19
Pp	20
Qq	22
Rr	23
Ss	24

Tt	
Uu	29
Vv	30
Ww	31
Xx Yy Zz	33
Numbers	34
Colours	35
Time words	36
Body words	38
Place words	39
Question words	39
Verbs	40
Story words	42
Feelings words	44
Opposites	45
My writing targets	46
My first 45 words	48
Other words I can spell	49

Aa

a

about

aeroplane

after

again

ago

air

airport

all

along

also

always

am

ambulance

an

and

angry

animal

another

any

apple

are

around

as

astronaut

at

ate

auntie

author

away

_____

_____

_____

_____

_____

_____

_____

_____

_____

_____

_____

_____

Bb

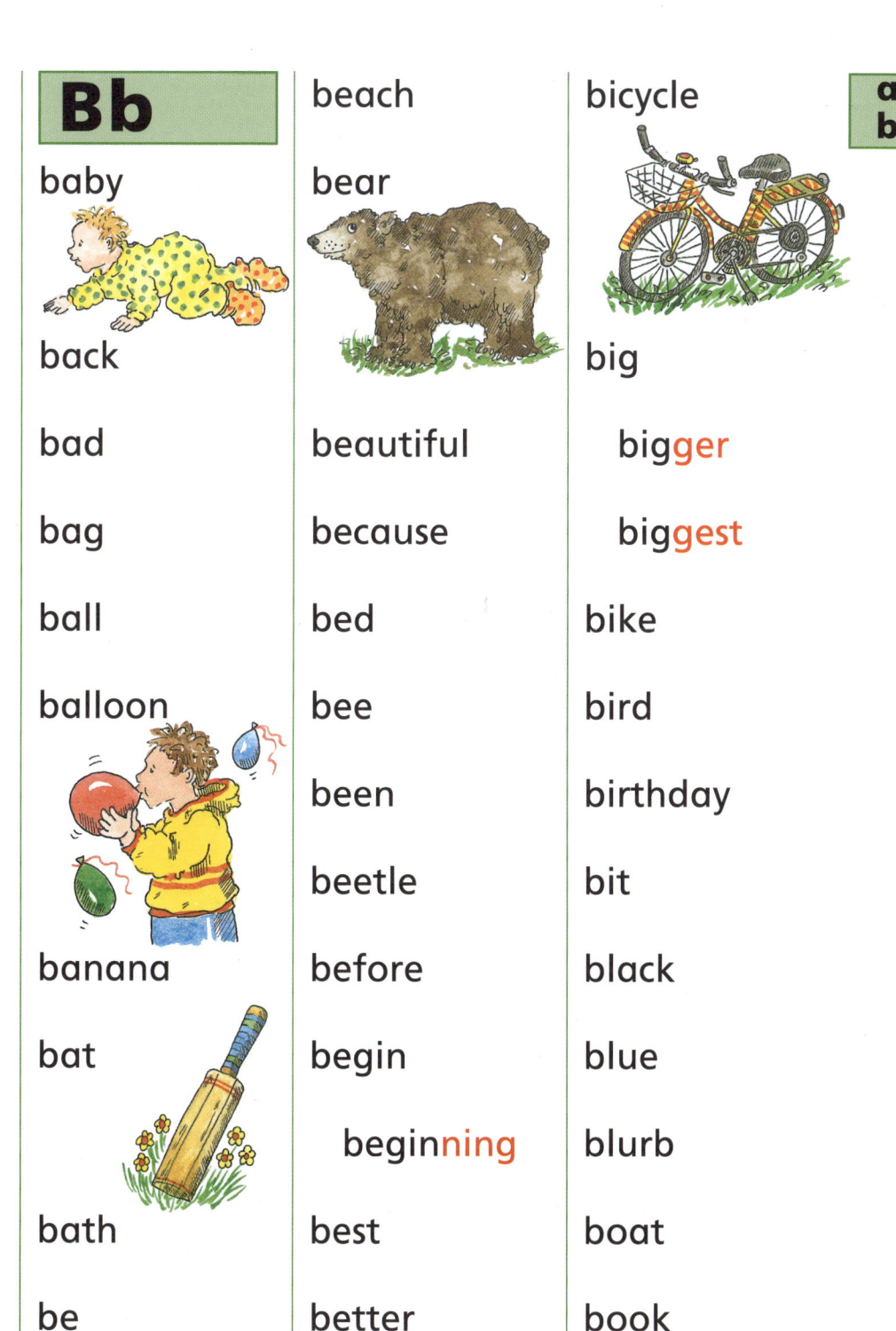

baby

back

bad

bag

ball

balloon

banana

bat

bath

be

beach

bear

beautiful

because

bed

bee

been

beetle

before

begin

begin**ning**

best

better

bicycle

big

big**ger**

big**gest**

bike

bird

birthday

bit

black

blue

blurb

boat

book

a
b

box

boy

brave

break

brother

brown

build

burger

bus

but

butterfly

buy

by

Cc

cake

came

camel

can

  can't

caption

car

card

careful

castle

cat

catch

caterpillar

centimetre (cm)

character

chicken

child

  children

chips

chocolate

church

circle

city

clean

clock

clothes

cloud

cloudy

clown

coat

cold

colour

come

  coming

comic	cry	
computer	cry**ing**	
contents	cube	
cook		
cook**ing**		
could		
could**n't**		
cover		
cow		
crab		
crayon		
crisps		
crocodile		

Dd

dad

   daddy

dance

dark

day

dear

deer

dictionary

did

   didn't

dig

dinner

dinosaur

disk

do

   don't

doctor

does

   doesn't

dog

doll

donkey

door

down

dragon

draw

dress

drink

duck

c
d

7

Ee

each

early

eat

   eat*ing*

egg

eight

eighteen

elephant

eleven

end

ever

every

   every*body*

   every*thing*

excited

   excit*ing*

eye

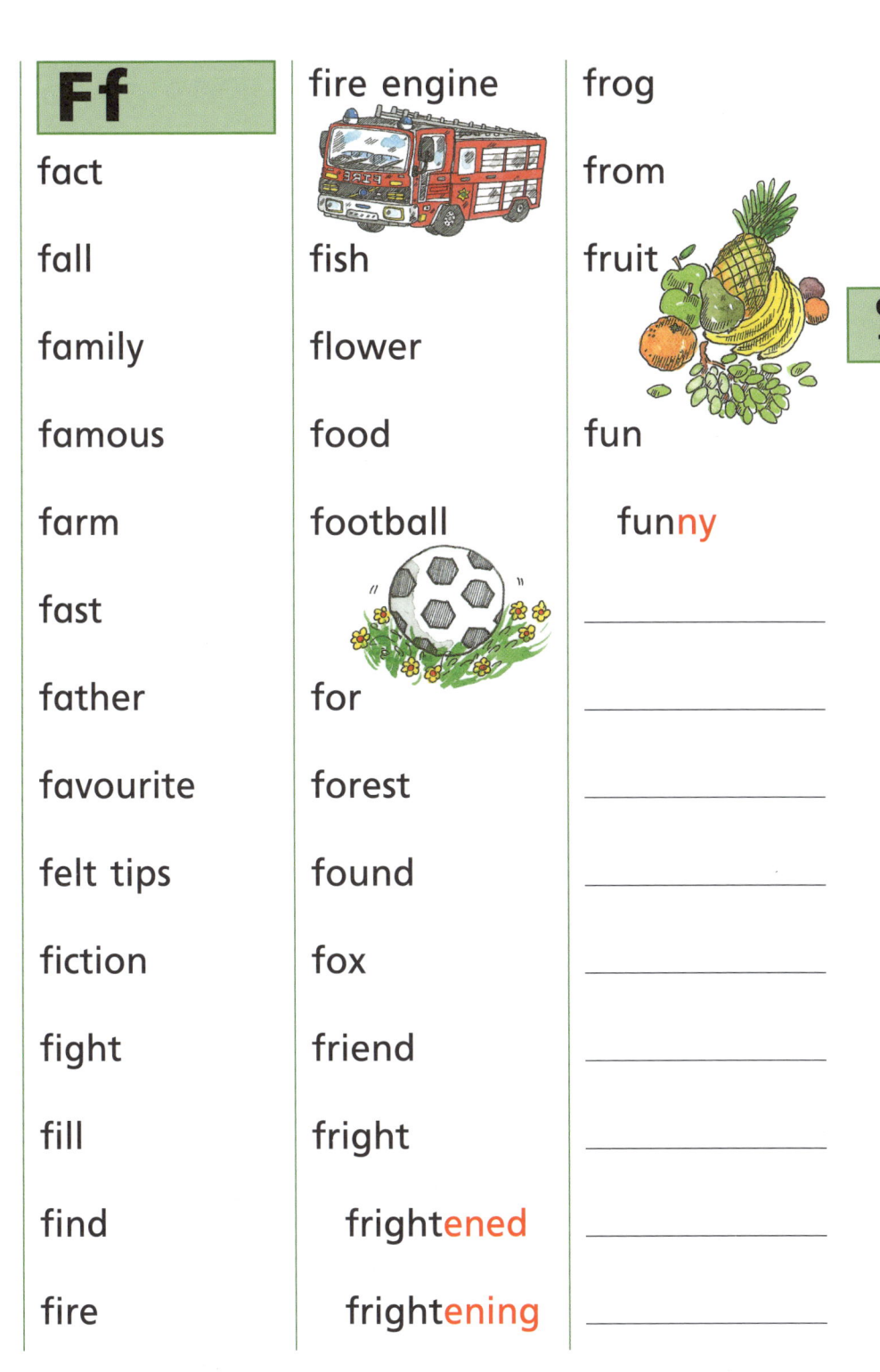

Ff	fire engine	frog
fact		from
fall	fish	fruit
family	flower	
famous	food	fun
farm	football	fun**ny**
fast		
father	for	
favourite	forest	
felt tips	found	
fiction	fox	
fight	friend	
fill	fright	
find	fright**ened**	
fire	fright**ening**	

e
f

Gg

game

garage

garden

gate

get

  get*ting*

ghost

giant

giraffe

girl

give

glossary

go

  go*es*

  go*ing*

goal

goat

good

gorilla

got

gran

grandma

grandpa

great

grow

growl

grumble

guess

_____

_____

_____

_____

_____

_____

_____

_____

_____

_____

_____

Hh

had

half

has

hat

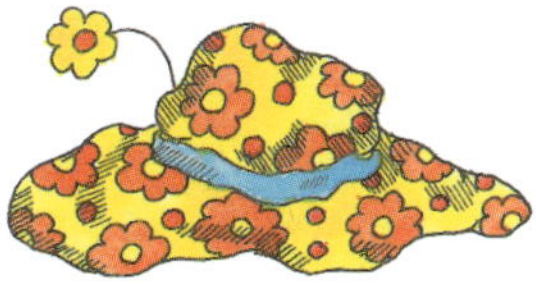

have

   have**n't**

   hav**ing**

he

heading

hear

heard

heavy

hedgehog

helicopter

help

hen

her

here

hill

him

his

hit

holiday

home

hop

hope

horror

horse

hospital

hot

hotel

house

hungry

hut

_____

_____

_____

_____

_____

g
h

Ii

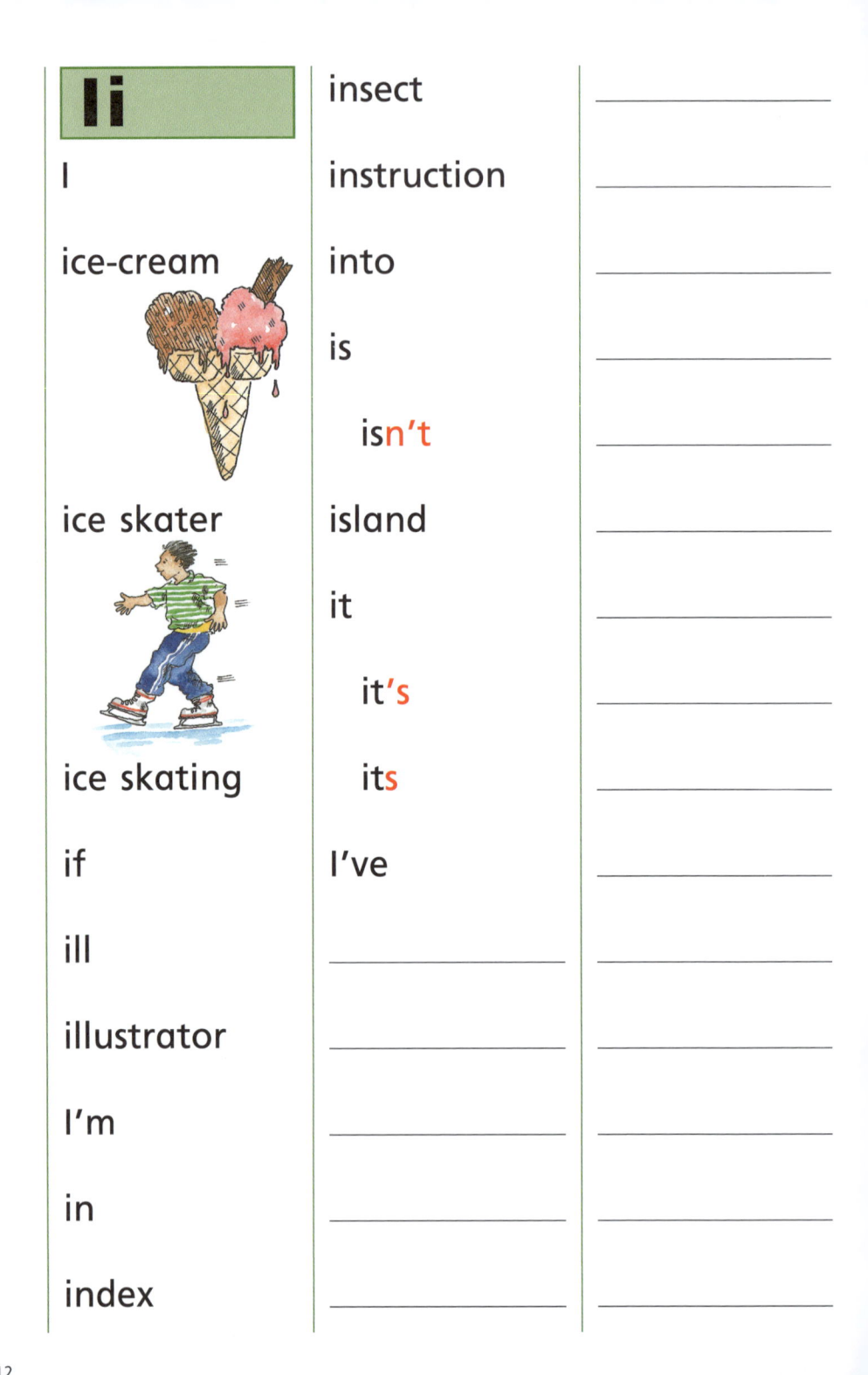

I

ice-cream

ice skater

ice skating

if

ill

illustrator

I'm

in

index

insect

instruction

into

is

   isn't

island

it

   it's

   its

I've

Jj

jacket

jam

jar

jeans

jelly

jigsaw

join

   joined

   joining

joke

juice

   juicy

   juicier

jump

   jumped

   jumper

   jumping

jungle

just

Kk

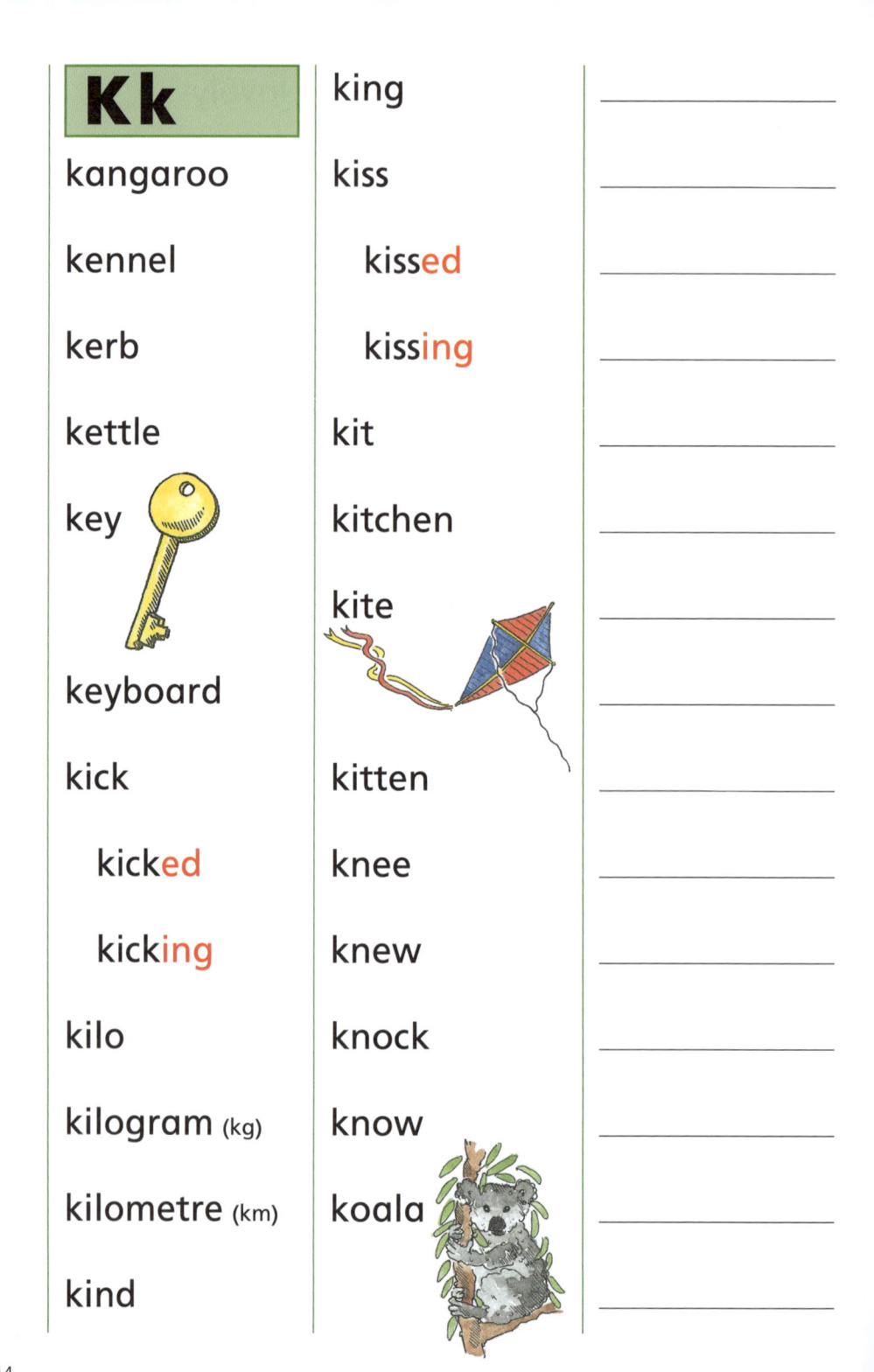

kangaroo

kennel

kerb

kettle

key

keyboard

kick

   kick**ed**

   kick**ing**

kilo

kilogram (kg)

kilometre (km)

kind

king

kiss

   kiss**ed**

   kiss**ing**

kit

kitchen

kite

kitten

knee

knew

knock

know

koala

Ll

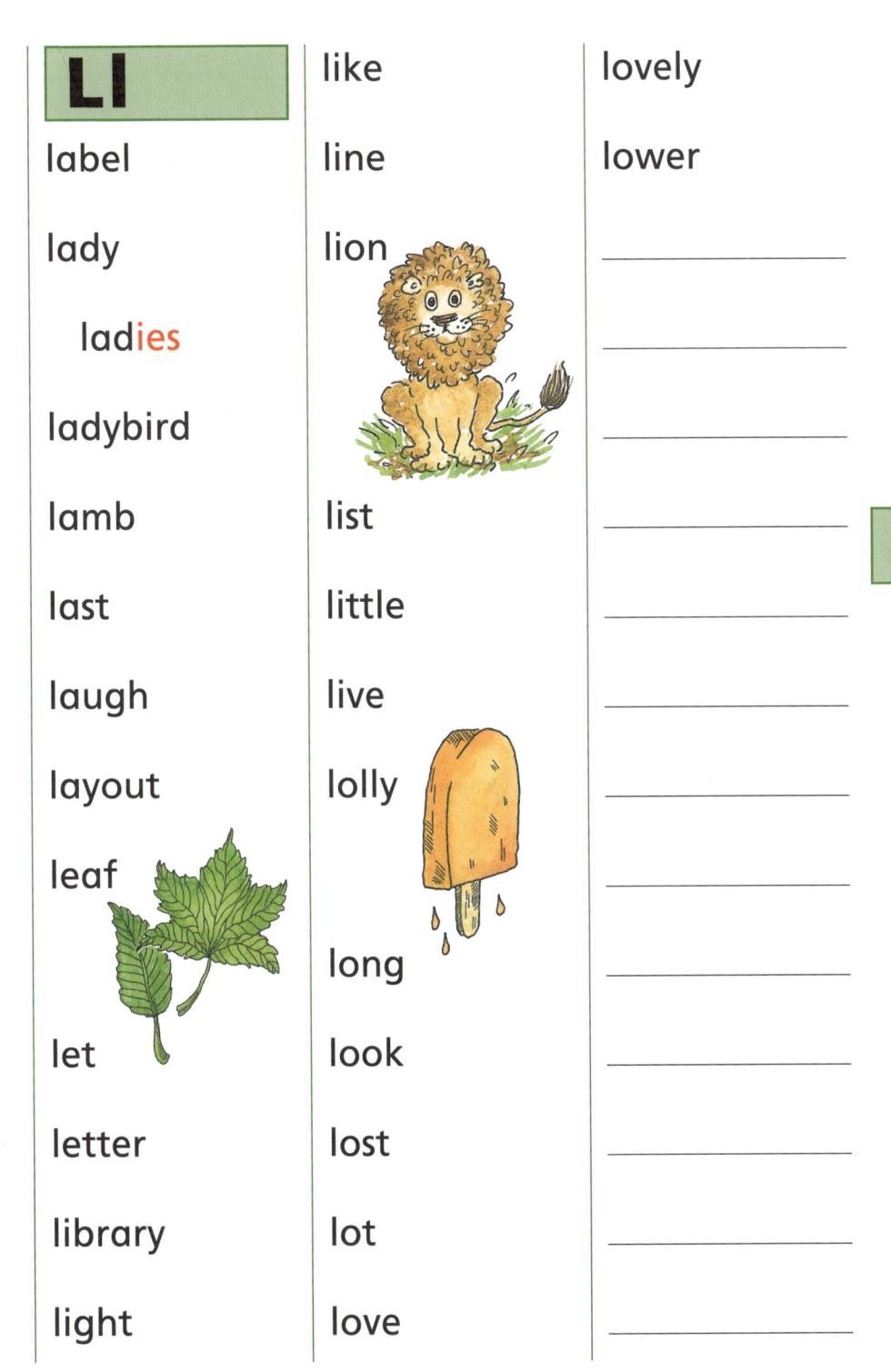

label

lady

   lad**ies**

ladybird

lamb

last

laugh

layout

leaf

let

letter

library

light

like

line

lion

list

little

live

lolly

long

look

lost

lot

love

lovely

lower

___

___

___

___

___

___

___

___

___

___

___

___

___

k
l

Mm

machine
made
magic
  magician
magnet
make
  making
man
many
market 
match
maths
may

me
measure
meet
men
metre (m)
mice 
might
milk
minibeast
minute
mix
mobile

money
monkey
monster 
month
moon
more
morning
mosque
most
moth
mother

motorbike

motorway

mountain

mouse

mouth

much

mum

   mum**my**

museum

music

must

my

m

Nn

name

naughty

near

   near*ly*

neighbour

nest

never

new

next

nice

night

nightie

nine

nineteen

no

non-fiction

nonsense

not

note

now

number

nurse

Oo

ocean

octopus

of

off

offer

old

on

once

one

only

onto

open

opposite

or

orange

orchestra

order

our

out

    out*side*

over

owl

own

owner

n
o

Pp

page

paint

   painted

   painting

palace

panda

paper

park

party

pen

pencil

penguin

people

phone

picture

pilot

pin

pink

pizza

place

planets

play

   played

   player

   playing

playground

playtime

please

   pleased

poem

poet

poetry

police

pony

poor

   poorly

present

pretty

prince

princess

print

problem

programme

pudding

pull

puppet

puppy

purple

push

   pushed

   pushing

put

puzzle

pyjamas

p

Qq

quack
   quack**ed**
   quack**ing**

quantity

quarter

queen

question

question mark

queue

quick
   quick**er**
   quick**ly**

quiet
   quiet**ly**

quit

quite

quiz

Rr

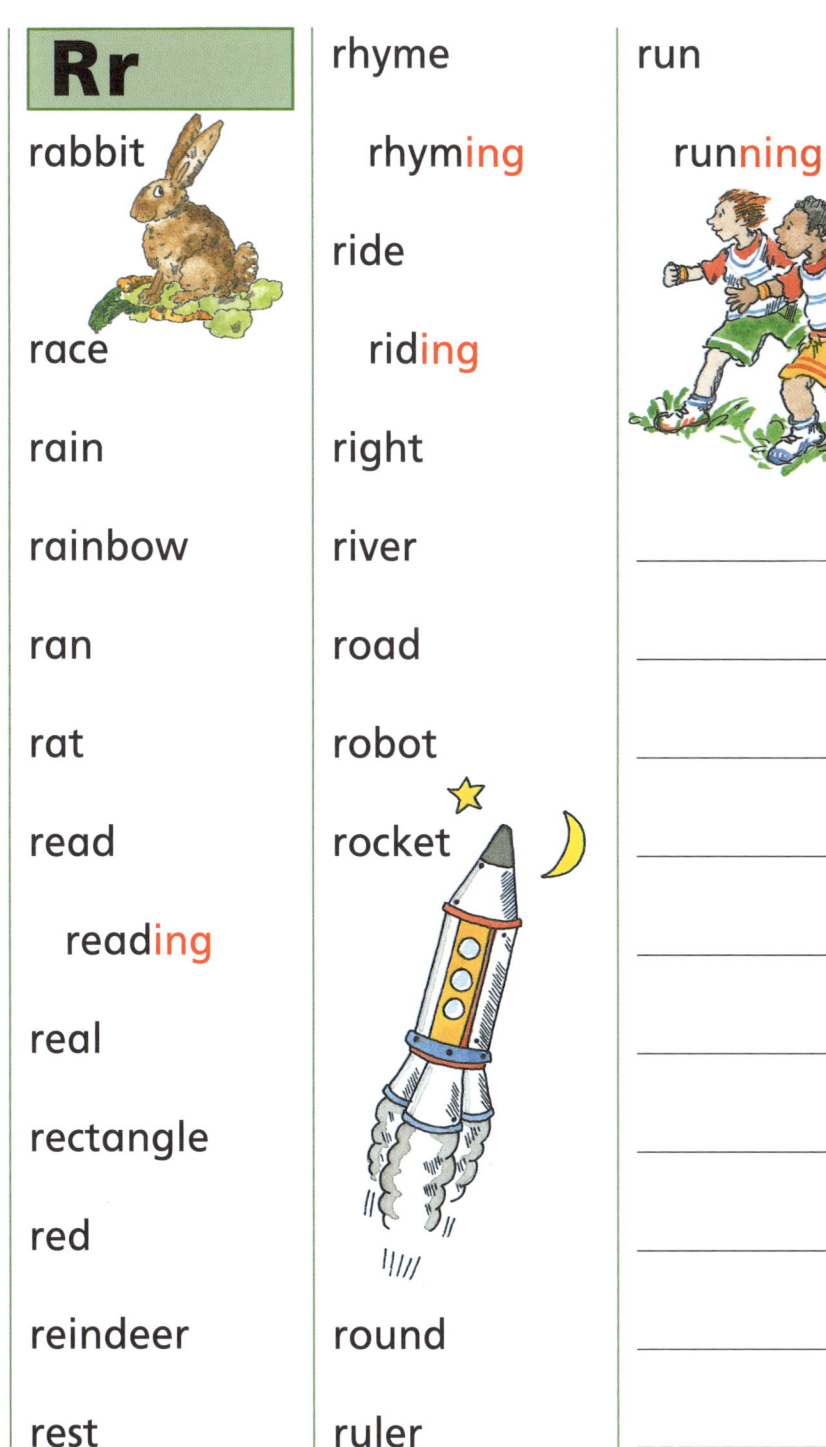

rabbit

race

rain

rainbow

ran

rat

read

   read*ing*

real

rectangle

red

reindeer

rest

rhyme

   rhym*ing*

ride

   rid*ing*

right

river

road

robot

rocket

round

ruler

run

   run*ning*

q
r

Ss

safari park

said

sailor

sand

sandcastle

sandwich

sari

sausages

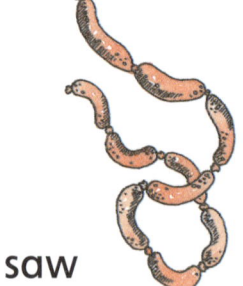

saw

say

say**ing**

scared

school

science

scissors

score

scream

sea

seal

seaside

secret

see

see**n**

seeds

sentence

set

set**ting**

shape

shark

sharp

she

sheep

shell

shiny

ship

shoe

shop	skeleton	so
shop*ped*	ski	soldier
shop*ping*	skull	some
short	sky	somersault
should	sleep	something
shout	slide	sometimes
shut	small	son
sick	smile	soon
sign	snail	sorry
silly	snake	sound
sing	snow	space
sister	snowman	speech
sit		spell
sit*ting*		spider
skate		spring

s

square

squirrel

star

start

station

stop

story

  stor**ies**

street

submarine

such

suddenly

sun

  sun**ny**

sunshine

supermarket

swan

sweets

swim

  swim**ming**

swing

synagogue

Tt

table

take

talk

tape

tea

teacher

team

teddy

teeth

telephone

television (TV)

tell

temple

tent

than

thank

that

the

their

them

then

there

these

they

thing

think

this

thought

through

throw

thunder

tiger

time

tiny

title

to

toadstool

s
t

today

toilet

told

tomorrow

too

took

tooth

tortoise

town

toys

tractor

train

trainers

treasure

tree

triangle

trousers

U u

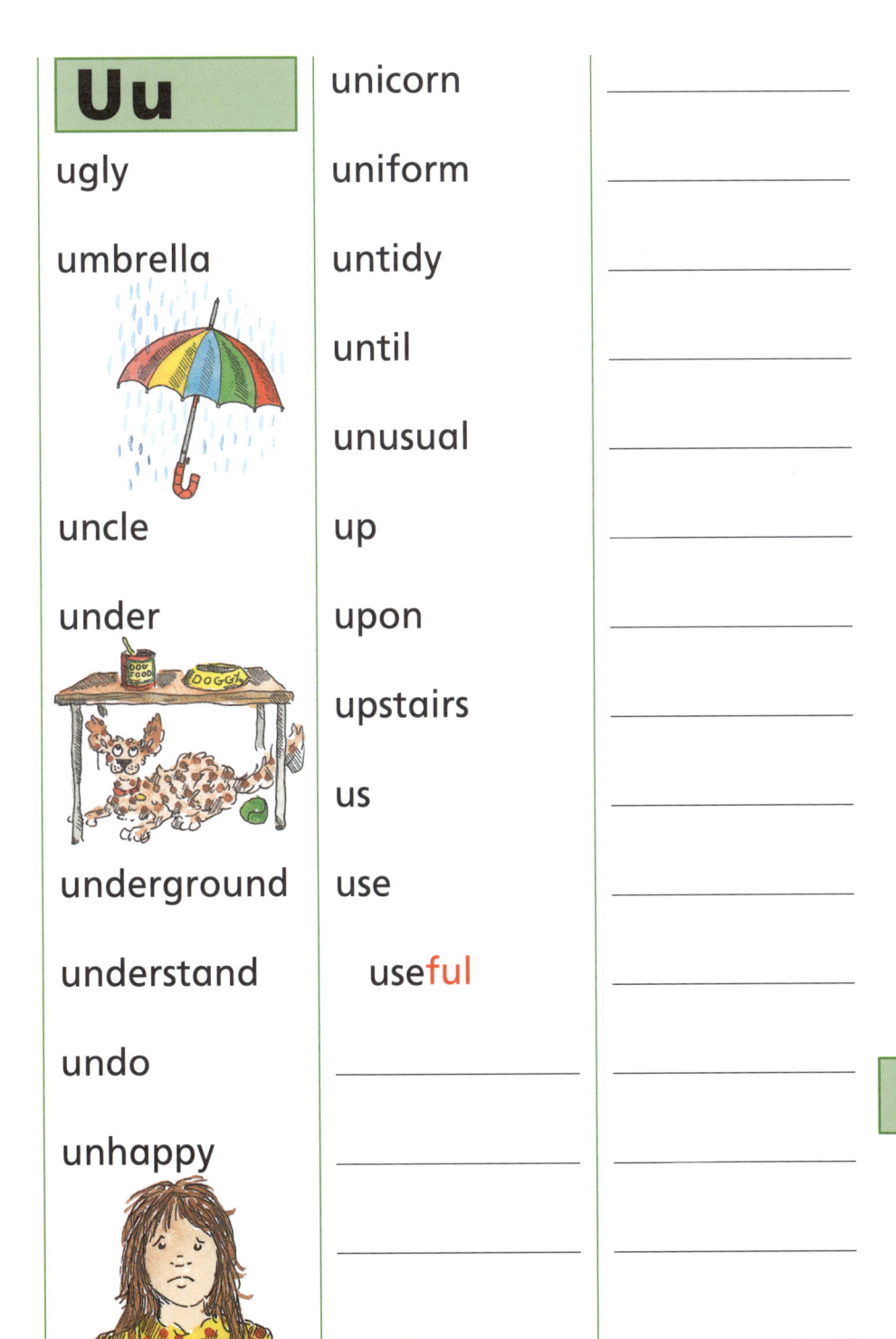

ugly

umbrella

uncle

under

underground

understand

undo

unhappy

unicorn

uniform

untidy

until

unusual

up

upon

upstairs

us

use

use**ful**

t
u

V v

van

vanish

   vanish**ing**

vegetables

vehicle

verse

very

vest

vet

video

view

village

violin

visit

   visit**ed**

   visit**ing**

voice

volcano

volume

voyage

vulture

W w

walk
- walked
- walking

want

warm

was

wash
- washed
- washing

wasp

watch
- watched
- watching

water

way

we

weather

week

weigh
- weighed
- weighing

well

wellingtons

went

were

wet

whale

what

wheel

when

where

which

while

white

who

why

will	woman	_____
win	wood	_____
wind	word	_____
window	work	_____
	world	_____
	worm	_____
wish	would	_____
wish**ed**	would**n't**	_____
wish**ing**	write	_____
witch	wrong	_____
	wrote	_____
with		_____
wizard		_____

Xx

x-ray

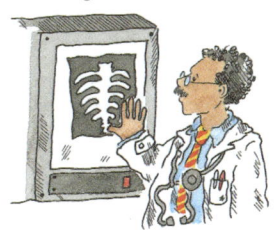

xylophone

_____

_____

_____

_____

_____

_____

_____

Yy

yacht

year

yell

yes

yet

yoghurt

you

young

your

_____

_____

_____

Zz

zebra

zebra crossing

zero

zip

zoo

_____

_____

_____

_____

_____

w
x
y
z

Numbers

0 zero	14 fourteen	100 one hundred
1 one	15 fifteen	
2 two	16 sixteen	thousand
3 three	17 seventeen	million
4 four	18 eighteen	1st first
5 five	19 nineteen	2nd second
6 six	20 twenty	3rd third
7 seven	30 thirty	4th fourth
8 eight	40 forty	5th fifth
9 nine	50 fifty	_____
10 ten	60 sixty	_____
11 eleven	70 seventy	_____
12 twelve	80 eighty	_____
13 thirteen	90 ninety	_____

Colours

Time words

Monday	January	day
Tuesday	February	week
Wednesday	March	month
Thursday	April	year
Friday	May	season
Saturday	June	calendar
Sunday	July	clock
	August	
spring	September	morning
summer	October	afternoon
autumn	November	evening
winter	December	night

today	quarter to	_____
yesterday		_____
tomorrow	birthday	_____
hour	holiday	_____
minute	festival	_____
second	Christmas	_____
midnight	Diwali	_____
	Easter	_____
o'clock	Eid-ul-Fitr	_____
	Hanukkah	_____
half past	Harvest	_____
	Id-al-Fitr	_____
quarter past	New Year	_____
	Ramadan	_____
	Yom Kippur	_____

Body words

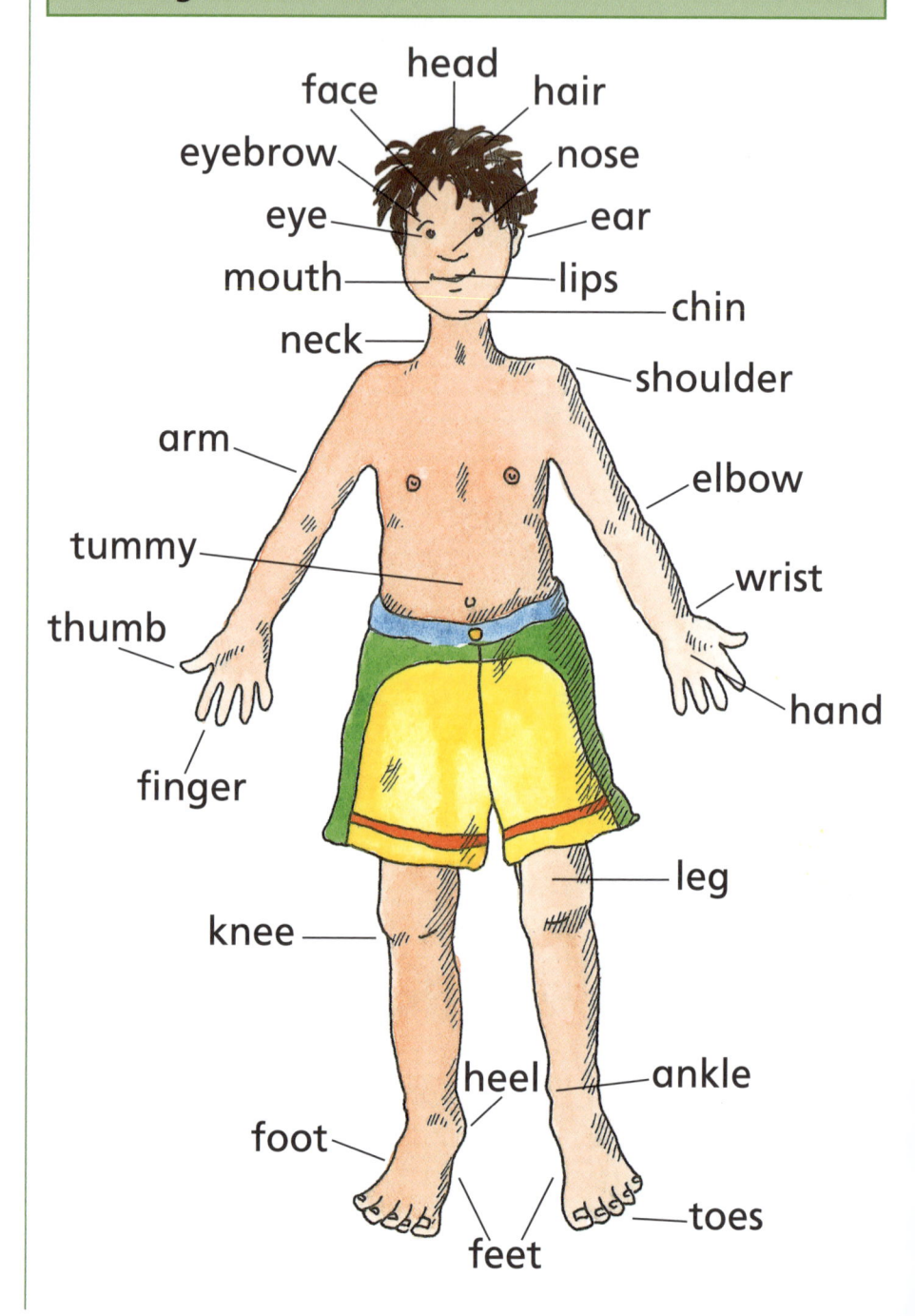

- head
- face
- hair
- eyebrow
- nose
- eye
- ear
- mouth
- lips
- chin
- neck
- shoulder
- arm
- elbow
- tummy
- wrist
- thumb
- hand
- finger
- leg
- knee
- heel
- ankle
- foot
- toes
- feet

Place words

above

behind

below

beside

between

in

inside

on

outside

over

through

under

Question words

how?

what?

which?

when?

where?

who?

why?

Verbs

answer

ask

  asked

  asking

bake

bend

blow

brush

carry

  carried

  carrying

choose

climb

crawl

cry

cut

cycle

dive

drag

  dragged

  dragging

drive

drop

feed

find

fly

hide

laugh

  laughed

  laughing

lie

lift

live

  lived

  living

mend

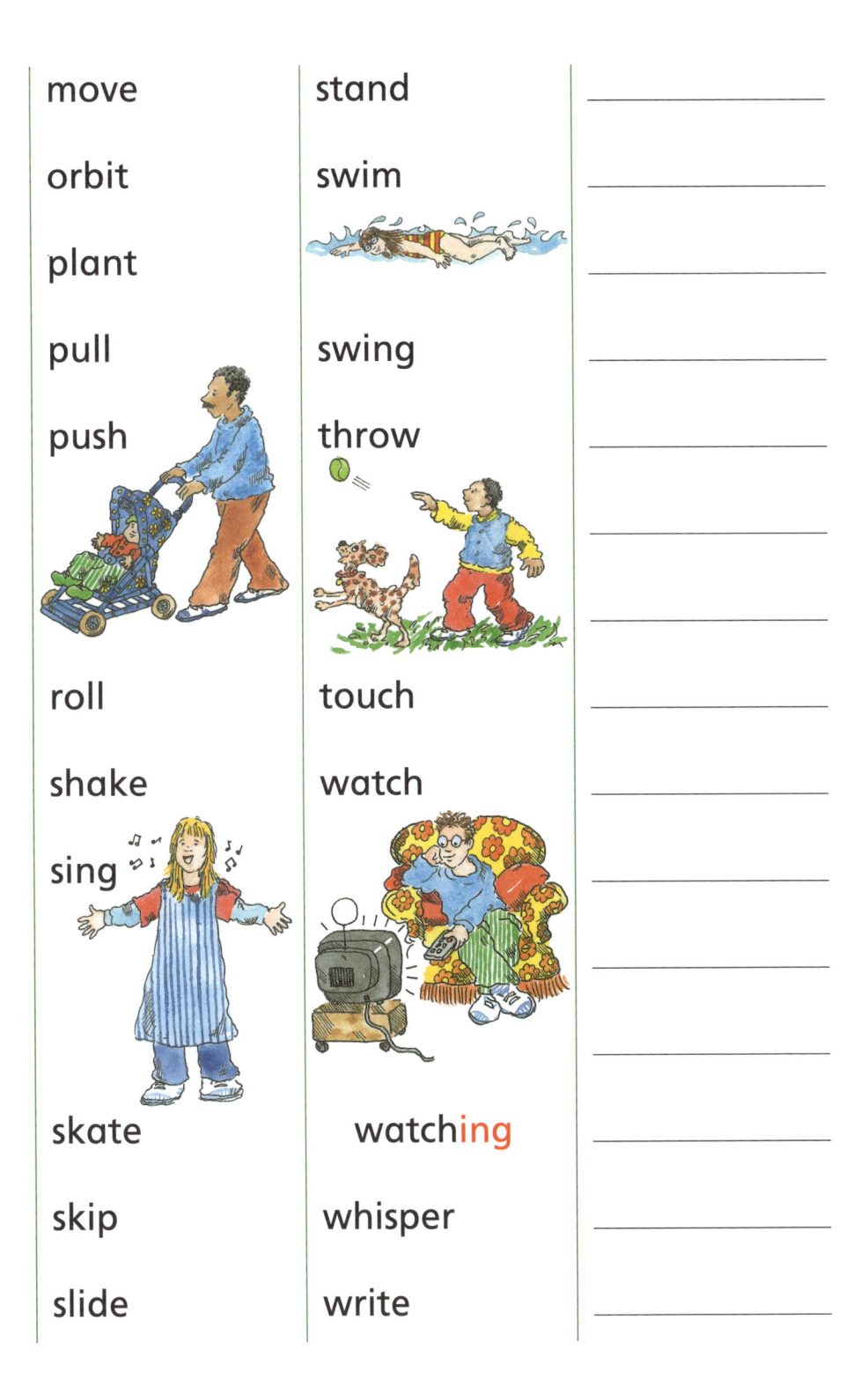

move	stand	_____
orbit	swim	_____
plant		_____
pull	swing	_____
push	throw	_____
		_____
roll	touch	_____
shake	watch	_____
sing		_____
		_____
skate	watch**ing**	_____
skip	whisper	_____
slide	write	_____

41

Story words

adventure	dragon	gold
ago	dwarf	happily
alien	elf	happy
bat	end	horrible
beginning	exciting	king
castle	fairy	knight
cauldron	frightening	
cave	frog	
chapter	funny	
characters	ghost	magic
cottage	giant	mermaid
	goblin	
danger		

monster	rhyme	wolf
mountain	rocket	
ogre	silver	
	spell	woods
	story	word
	stor**ies**	_____
once	title	_____
palace	treasure	_____
pirate		_____
		_____
	troll	_____
poem	wand	_____
prince	wicked	_____
princess	witch	_____
queen	wizard	_____

Feelings words

angry	full	safe
bad	good	shy
bored	happy	sick
bossy	helpful	silly
brave	hot	sore
calm	hungry	sorry
clean	hurt	sulky
cold	ill	tearful
comfortable	lonely	thirsty
dirty	naughty	tired
disappointed	nervous	uncomfortable
dry	pleased	warm
envious	relaxed	well
excited	restless	wet
frightened	sad	worried

Opposites

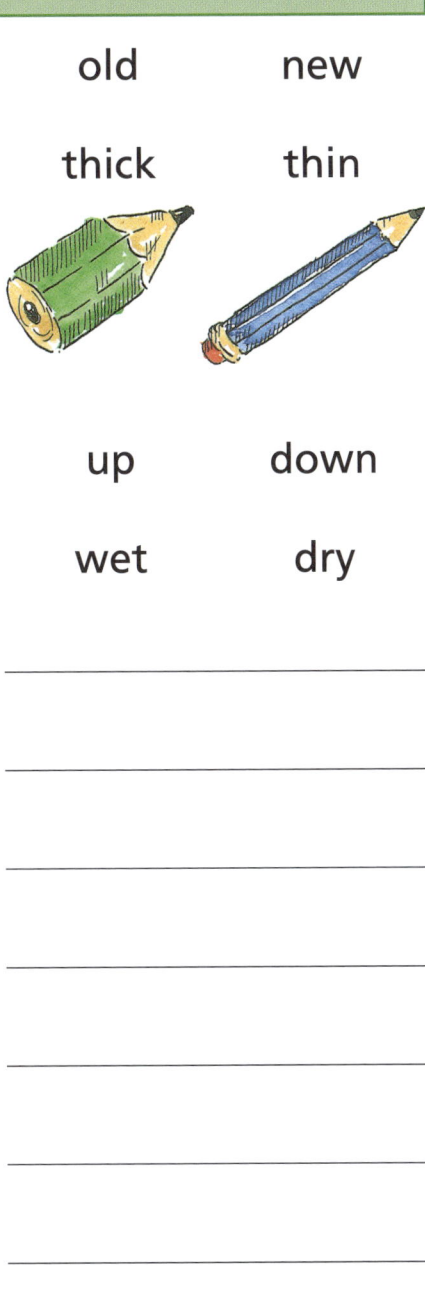

big	small	old	new
clean	dirty	thick	thin
dark	light	up	down
fast	slow	wet	dry
happy	sad		
hot	cold		
long	short		

45

My writing targets

Date set	Target

Adult's comments	Date met

My first 45 words

the	is	what
and	for	there
a	at	out
to	his	this
said	but	have
in	that	went
he	with	be
I	all	like
of	we	some
it	can	so
was	are	not
you	up	then
they	had	were
on	my	go
she	her	little